Black Sheep

Wattney Lander

Black Sheep

Copyright © 2023 Wattney Lander

All rights reserved. No part of this book may be used or reproduced in any form without prior written permission from the author, except in the case of brief quotations in a book review or scholarly journal.

ISBN: 978-1-7388416-0-8

www.wattneypoetry.com

Wattney Lander

To my readers

This is your time to remember who you are
and embrace the galaxy you hold within
yourself.

To Stone and Hart

May you always notice the beauty within your storms.
And remember the magic held within your names.

I love you both so very much.

Black Sheep

Let's begin, again

They stood still
and never moved
out of that house
that filled them with pain
because they were frightened of the unknown
and got comfortable with knowing
what to expect

- Existence is bigger than four walls

Black Sheep

Sometimes
when others tell me
they feel alone
I start to think that
it's not nice to hear
but it's comfortable to know

- That makes two of us

She was swallowed
by an avalanche
defeated by rough waters
and suffered in silence
but she stood in front of me
and I just knew
I was introduced
to the most beautiful girl
in the world

- Beautiful people don't just happen

Black Sheep

Your anger was proof
that you haven't healed
so instead of looking at me
as the problem
clean out your wounds
and forgive yourself
for holding onto something
for far too long

- Inner battles

Just because I didn't speak
doesn't mean I didn't say anything

- Energy makes noise too

Black Sheep

Sometimes
I don't want to write down
how I truly feel
because having it said
outside of my mind
means the words could travel
and I'll have a lot of explaining to do

Wattney Lander

She jumped the flames
you hoped would burn her
dodged the rocks
that tried to hit her
and drank the water
you used to drown her
what did you expect
when you planted seeds in her name?

- Wildflower

Black Sheep

When I'm alone
I pretend who I want to be
but with them
I'm stuck with who
I really am

Wattney Lander

It was the rain that nurtured my soul
washed me of all my sorrows
and fed me hope when I was weak

Black Sheep

You could've helped me heal
but fear got the best of you
so here I go
trying to forgive with no explantation

- This one will take time

Wattney Lander

The walls are tarnished
with the reminders of what happened
and no matter how many times
you try to repaint them
It will never cover up the stories
It's stained too deep

- Broken home

Black Sheep

She was doing everything in her power
to shed light on something
that was kept hidden in the dark
to awaken them from living in ignorance and bliss
and save the soul who needed it the most

- Can you hear me now?

Wattney Lander

There are some
that have layers
of unreleased pain
gathered in their soul
and though they have the choice to heal
and set themselves free
most choose not to let it go

Black Sheep

They judged
her methods
but applauded
her madness

She was never the one
to stay within the borders
of your expectations
and by forcing her to stay
ended up becoming
the biggest mistake
of your life

- No second chances

Black Sheep

I was left
to pick up the pieces
but it was then that I learned
there was something beautiful
about a broken picture
it gives your pain a purpose
and it also sets you free

Wattney Lander

It's one of the worst feelings
knowing that I finally rose
from the burning torment I was in
and then when at liberty
I'm a wandering puppy

I can't wait till I find my world
sit there and feel
this is where I belonged all along

Black Sheep

She was finding it hard
to love someone
that she desperately wanted
to feel love from

Wattney Lander

Call her the outcast
the one that finally spoke
to break the routine
of projecting emotional baggage
onto our children
to give them a chance
to thrive as their unique selves
instead of being programmed to be
just like their parents

Black Sheep

They said my words
were hurting them
but I knew the pain
they were holding onto
was hurting them more

I couldn't live to believe
"This is the way it is" anymore
I was hungry for life
I needed to feel
the thrill of the chase
and capture what I knew
was always meant for me
regardless of what they kept saying
and I guess that's how you start to feel
when you finally leave the herd
and start becoming friends
with wolves

- Black Sheep

Black Sheep

Her muscles
will heal from the pain
but her bones
will never forget

It's not until they realize
all you were trying to do
was to show them a way out
of all this misery
that they begin to embrace your time
and thoughts
and eventually thank you
for being the one
to wake up too

- And hopefully they do

Black Sheep

Going through moments and memories
I can write and articulate
dozens of times, places and scenes
but there's no point, and it's a waste to echo
when you wouldn't comprehend it anyway

- They will only ever see it from their perspective

Wattney Lander

She was never afraid of darkness
for it gave her a moment to breathe
silence to ponder her dreams
and the chance to find and follow her heart

She may have been given
the love the way they knew how
but it wasn't given in the way
she needed to feel it

- Love languages

Wattney Lander

You told everyone
we were
over the moon
when actually
I was
walking along the edge

Black Sheep

When they're bothered
by just your presence
it's because you constantly remind them
of the things they buried so deep down
that every time they see your face
all those things immediately hit the surface
and they can no longer keep it a secret

- Truth always finds a way out

Wattney Lander

They're just trying to
brainwash you
into thinking the way
you love is wrong
ignore them
and love the way
your heart tells you to

Black Sheep

She dissected issues
like swallowing pills
thinking it would heal her
when it just slowly stopped her heart
from ever feeling again

Wattney Lander

They told me
my mind
couldn't stay on track
I told them
it's because I lead
with my heart

Black Sheep

I thought it was going to take
a world journey
to total my hunches and starvation
when in reality, it all happened
within a juncture of captured sayings
and it's growth over my head
within my own home

- When you wake up

They tried so hard
to read her
but no one could ever hold her
like the wind
she was constantly moving
thinking
and doing
things they didn't and won't ever
understand

- Dance to the beat of your own drum

Black Sheep

Sometimes
we have to speak out
to fully understand
what is inside of you
that needs and wants
to get out

Wattney Lander

Holding onto your past stories
robs you of your future
and kills the thoughts
that you can move on from it

Black Sheep

When you yell at me
I smile inside
because I know
it's actually you
yelling at yourself
it's never my fault
it's just you
hating yourself
for the actions that you didn't take
when you were supposed to take them
or bundled up negative memories
that you haven't yet healed from

- Young but wise

Wattney Lander

They tried to read
as many books
to figure out
what she was
but they'll never find her
within the pages
she's magic

She was the home
where the ghosts felt
comfortable enough
to stay

- Living and dead

Wattney Lander

She held onto the pain
like the earth holds onto water
creating oceans so large
that she would begin to weep
out of the blue
and forget all the reasons
why she overflowed
in the first place

Black Sheep

You didn't show up
to hear me
you came here
to listen to yourself

- Actions speak louder than words

Wattney Lander

She'll remember
the good things
you did for her
but it will never
make her erase
the shitty things
you put her through

Black Sheep

I would do anything
and have tried
to hold a relationship with you
but I discovered it wasn't easy
for a tree to grow
on land that's been burnt
by a generational forest fire

- But nature always finds a way

You think therapy
is going to destroy this family
this family was already destroyed
by guilting the children into believing
thats what true love looked like

Black Sheep

Be aware
that sometimes
when others
compliment you
it could only be
to feed your mind
into believing
that you are moving
through life
when in reality
they see you're stuck
and want you
to keep living that way

- Just so they could get ahead

Wattney Lander

I fell in love
with the way
I was quiet
and how I was all alone
because during that time
my intuition's voice became louder
and I was able to call myself home

Being clenched in a station
that is more than you can conduct
is a dream propelled in a spider web
just wanting to be free
or waiting to be eaten
with a crunch

I left too many messages
to the point of exhaustion
and I realized
it wasn't my fault
or responsibility
that you didn't follow
or pick them up clearly

- The signs were there

Black Sheep

For years
I wasn't able to think
I couldn't function
in the way society told me to
I was frozen
paralyzed
Because that's what begins to happen
when you lose someone
and I remember
it only hit me
after an old friend
told me what was going on
she read everything
in my mind, that was hidden
and she read it
off of my face
like it was printed
in perfect ink
on my forehead

- Real friends tell the truth, even if it hurts

Wattney Lander

I hope there comes a time
when we can sit
across from one another
and recognize
how similar we are
and understand
your story is my story

Black Sheep

Your hurricane
may have destroyed my body
but it wasn't strong enough
to change my mind

I have done
all that I could
and all that I can
but seeing how situations
are handled
I'd rather give myself
a moment to be proud of
then wait to hear the reasons
you left me with

- Your time is valuable, don't waste it

Not telling your children
what's going on
creates more damage
than telling them the truth
about your life

- Things catch up, be honest

Wattney Lander

I was constantly pushed away
but then always told to say
"I love you" back

- I thought love was more about giving than taking

Black Sheep

They may have created your body
blood and bones
but you design your soul
a part of you in which
no one can ever keep

Wattney Lander

A name doesn't make you family
love does

Black Sheep

I know what it's like
to never finish a love story
the mystery follows your mind
and you stay confident in your "one day"

- One day he'll come back...

Wattney Lander

"You can't save everyone"

"You're right; you can't.
But you can at least try
until there are no more chances."

- Not giving up

Black Sheep

The love you need exists
just let go
of the thought
that it's not available

Wattney Lander

And then the day came
when you left
and I could finally see
what was always hidden
behind those mountains

- Freedom

Black Sheep

Don't lie to me
I can tell
cause your energy
starts saying more
than your mouth does

Wattney Lander

You can't force people
To face their problems
When they aren't ready to

Black Sheep

It doesn't matter
the age of the person hurting
they're hurting

Wattney Lander

It's a helpless feeling
when you see them hurting
but you can't take it away
all I do is pray

Black Sheep

I wish you could heal yourself
so we'd have a better relationship

Wattney Lander

I had to shake your ground
to get you to understand
you were never as sturdy
as you thought you once were
and to show you
a stacked deck of cards
doesn't make for a good home

Black Sheep

When I sent you a text
you applied your own tone to it
misunderstanding my words
and creating issues
that were never there

Wattney Lander

Some days
I live amongst my darkness
as I allow it to paint
my whole entire sky
and though it's here
I still discover friends
who will meet me
in the fog

Black Sheep

When I was a kid
and I fought with my parents
I would hide in my room
with my back pressed against the door
so no one could come in
and I would cry asking myself
"why was I put here?"

Wattney Lander

The day I said
"No" to you
is the day
I finally met
who you really are

Black Sheep

All your actions
just remind me
of all the things
they won't need
to recover from

Wattney Lander

They wanted to show me
what was best for me
so much so
that they grabbed
every other piece
of information and hid it
for me to think
there was only one way
to live the life I wanted
but the best thing
about being a black sheep is
we eventually find the truth
and we can always see behind
your pretty little lies

Black Sheep

They tried to dig our graves
place us in the ground
to show others
that what we know
has no truth
and it's only when
we started to prove ourselves
that they began
throwing the dirt

Wattney Lander

Once is an accident
twice is not a mistake

Black Sheep

Recording my words
just shows that you do not trust me
and you constantly want
to prove to others
that your story is the truth
but trying to prove to others
that there is damage
on your skin
is just your way
of building a team
against a fight
that you're too afraid
to face alone

Wattney Lander

Our relationship
was bruised once again
but this time
to help wounds heal
I had to place boundaries down
and it's not to try
and hurt you
it's so we can try
to continue
this relationship together
in a respectful way

Black Sheep

They all fought
to be the first to hold information
to the point where
they didn't even care
if it held the truth

- do you see it yet?

Wattney Lander

I had questions
I didn't follow their lead
and now that the dust has settled
they're apologizing
for not listening to me sooner

Black Sheep

I was the only one
who had the strength
to fall backwards
completely trusting gravity
and believing in my own wings

Wattney Lander

They have made us look like
the uneducated ones
for standing up
for ourselves
but remember
eventually
everything comes full circle
and nothing
can stop our voices
from echoing
nothing can hold back
the sounds of the truth

Black Sheep

I am tired
of keeping my hand
over my mouth

- facts will set you free

Wattney Lander

Thank you
for cutting me open
I can finally breathe

She shifted
Her thoughts and beliefs from
"I need fixing"
and
" I'm not good enough"
to
"I will be seen"
" I will be heard"
and
"I will love her…
just as I am"
"I will love this woman"

- path to self love

Wattney Lander

I am building the woman
I know I am destined to be
my old habits and routines
are drifting
and freeing the layers of questions
I thought I needed the answers to
but I am building her
and I am doing it
for me

Black Sheep

You've walked many life times
decide today that this will be the one
that will take you to the places of healing
so you no longer repeat
the heaviness in your heart
time after time

Wattney Lander

As I get older
I start to recognize
that people will start
to talk about things
when they're open
to changing it

Black Sheep

Hey
you can't save them
from their pain
by continuing
to lift it
on your back
for them

Wattney Lander

Just when I thought
I knew the reason why I chose you
a whole new reason
came along
and that taught me
to never settle
in what you know
and always be open
to more than
what is expected

Black Sheep

You may be feeling
like the rough currents
and tidal waves of life
are pulling you under
but trust the buoyancy
of your body
it's yours to teach you
that no matter how many times
you think you're drowning
you do have the choice to rise
and welcome yourself
back to shore

- you have the power to be on top of it all

Wattney Lander

You can let your story
of sadness own you
control you
or you can recycle it
to heal yourself
and others too

Black Sheep

They warned her
about the other side
never enter and to stay
within the grass-cut lines
but one day, she leaned in
regardless of the fear
they soaked her with
and by taking that first step
she birthed a new cycle for the future
to always go where
your soul is being called
and never fit into moulds
that were sculpted by others

Wattney Lander

Sometimes
your beginnings
will actually be endings
that you'll have to go through
over and over again
to eventually realize
it will never be
a "meant to be" story

- Insanity

Black Sheep

If you were to look
On my life map
it would have "how"
written all over it

"How would I do this? How would I get there?"

As if I needed specific directions
then I remembered
when birds fly south for the winter
they just go
and they make it there
every time
so here I go
trusting my intuition

- Fuck the map

Wattney Lander

She was raised to believe
that wings weren't used for flying
until one day, she fell
off of the mountain of words
that was pushed on her
and flew 29 years away
for a fresh start
in trusting her own strength

- Believe in yourself

Black Sheep

I realized that your loss
was my push
and made me create wonderful things
within myself
I was supposed to lose you in order
for myself to grow in ways, I wouldn't before

Wattney Lander

Here's to the women
that had the strength
to lift the roots
from underneath them
and plant their wounded hearts
facing a new light

Black Sheep

I planted a garden
directly on the paths
taken by the ones before me
because there was no need
to repeat those steps
and continue the heartbreak
between a mother and daughter relationship

- Change is coming

Wattney Lander

I never lost anything
I gained my life back
my ambience is so utopian
without you in it
and now, when I breathe out
the compressed sensitivity will float away
attention to try and forgive
but never forget
to rid out the trolls
and keep the vortex of my kinship
safe and close by

Black Sheep

If you feel like you're only being included
when it's convenient for them
walk away and shift your energy elsewhere
your intuition is never wrong
and above everything
your time here is worth more
than being settled in a one-sided relationship

When you will never receive
the love you need
because, unfortunately, they're
holding onto past traumas
know you can always find that love
in someone else
no need to wait around
when a healing
will never reach the surface

- Pray for them though

Black Sheep

And instead of things falling apart in the end
I glued new pieces together
and paved my own walkway home
instead of following the old broken one

- Picking up what's left of me

Wattney Lander

There will come a time
when you will need to remove yourself
from a toxic relationship
and sometimes to protect yourself
you will want to burn the bridge
and the whole fucking path
leading up to it

do it

because nothing is better
then living a life
free from chains

Black Sheep

Stay close to those
who bring you back
to the simple ingredients of life
how we should be thankful for living
and stop doubting our reasons
for being here

- Once you find them, don't let them go

She saw the signs
but she ignored them
because having something
and being able to
hold onto it
for just a little while longer
was better than having
absolutely
nothing at all

- can't surrender just yet

Black Sheep

As more of the pages are being flipped over
it starts to create visions in my head
of why everything happens for a reason
becomes so true

and now I smile everyday
because I know I deserve to

Wattney Lander

The best way
to change yourself
is to know yourself
so dive in deep
through the swamp and clear waters
and say hello
to the person
you've been hiding all along

Black Sheep

Without pain

I wouldn't love the way I do
wouldn't have grown the way I have
and wouldn't have used my voice
the way I am
I was meant for you
you were meant for me

- Grateful heart

Wattney Lander

Eventually
she stopped settling
for paved paths
and finally started thinking
for herself
it's only then that she discovered
how far she could reach for the stars
and become who and what
she was meant to be
with no one else
holding her hand

Black Sheep

She allowed her garden
to bloom the way
it was destined to
with weeds, bugs and worms
to teach her daughter
that everything living
deserves love
and the chance to love too

- You're perfect, just the way you are

Seek yourself
and once you find her

tell her it's okay
to heal from past wounds

tell her its safe
to let go of the pain

and tell her she's home
and at last, we can jump the flames

Black Sheep

It's always good to wonder
but sometimes
the answer is not for you to hold

Wattney Lander

She kept him close
knowing that nothing
was for certain
but the time spent together
was so worth it
for he gave her
what no one else had
hope

Black Sheep

You were
the greatest teacher of all
someone I had to face and forgive
so that I could release my heavy heart
and no longer live
with chains bolted to the ground

- Healing is your responsibility

Wattney Lander

Surround and welcome yourself
with others that are on
different life paths than you
so together, you can destroy
all cultural conditioning
and relearn the true meaning
of life

Black Sheep

To some
it's another day
a unit of time
held within 24 hours
to me
it's evidence that I survived
two years without you

- And I'm okay

Wattney Lander

She never knew why
she didn't write about him
until she looked at herself
and realized
true love didn't need a pen and paper
it existed on its own
with the fingerprints
he left on her skin

Sharing our gifts with the world
brings education to some
and a reason to push forward
for others

Fears are just blocks of proof
proof that you can face them
and what's behind fear
is certainly a freedom
a freedom which you have always wanted
and I finally got mine

- You can overcome a n y t h i n g

Black Sheep

The oldest trees
are wise enough to know
whether or not they get hit
by lightning during a storm
they will still live a strong
and healthy life
for they know
earth would never give up
on the roots they planted
in her soul

I miss us being together
but all I have to do
are close my eyes
close my eyes
and you're right there

- Separation is only an illusion

Black Sheep

If you're lost
search for yourself
once you do that
you'll be able to find anything
including a home

- Even if the home is held within yourself

Enjoy the waiting game
celebrate it instead of
watering anger and jealousy
know that you'll appreciate it more
once it arrives

Most of the time
having instant gratification
just makes those things
worth less in the end

- It's always worth the wait

Black Sheep

We were proof
that when it came to love
labels didn't matter
and it never should

Wattney Lander

You're the one
that made me believe
my thoughts were real
and not just imaginary

- Let the dreamer dream

Black Sheep

Stop sitting on the floor
with everyone else
establish your boundaries
set the environment
for them to understand
you're a leader
and take a seat in your chair

Wattney Lander

She fast forwarded
her world
only to realize
life was worth
living on pause

Black Sheep

Sometimes
when we make changes
it's actually for the next relationship
and not the one
you're currently in

Wattney Lander

It took all the strength
she had
to forgive the one
who took away
her proudest moments

- Forgive but never forget

Black Sheep

I could've let you
come back
but I'm not going to
abandon myself
anymore

- Take care of yourself first

Wattney Lander

Your arrow may take
many paths to hit the bullseye
be proud of that
nobody likes a perfect story

Black Sheep

You could've woken up to realize
that the pain you've been fighting
came from family roots
and the only way to stop it
is if you're ready to heal it
within your soul

Know that this is the kind of battle
you fight with no weapons but deep love
and you do it to stop the poison
from leaking onto the hearts
of the new and unborn souls

- Break the curse in this lifetime

Wattney Lander

You may not end up together
forever
but you'll certainly
light up each other's way
back home

- Look on the bright side

Black Sheep

She never responded
to those that yelled at her
in hopes that they would
hear themselves
and understand
rage isn't the answer

Wattney Lander

Allow the hurt
to help you
look at the world
with open eyes
breathe with a brave heart
and think with a wise mind

Forgiving
didn't start with them
It didn't begin when they changed
their actions
forgiving started
when I forgave myself
for holding onto those moments
of the past
and stopped projecting it
into my future
on replay

- It starts with you. With us. Forgive yourself for holding too much

Wattney Lander

She was strong enough
to notice the damage
and rejuvenate it
with a peaceful heart
so that she could
raise her children
far from the world
she once belonged too

Tears
were meant to exit the body
and if they don't
you won't grow into
who you're supposed to be

- Let it out, water your soul

Wattney Lander

Embrace change
sometimes it leads you
to where you're supposed to be
the paths are hard
but what's waiting for you
is exactly what you've wanted
all along

Black Sheep

If they still want to leave
after all that
let them
let them, go

Maybe
they aren't conscious
of the salt
they're pouring
in your wounds
but they are
when they tell you
it's sugar

Black Sheep

The day you left
without a choice
was one of the hardest moments
in my life
but it was also the day
I finally came home
to myself

- there's always a light in every storm

Wattney Lander

Exhale, love
holding your breath
won't make it go away

Nothing is more beautiful
than the strength it takes
to see you rise

Wattney Lander

There she was
in the middle of nowhere
holding her breath
so she could only hear
the stillness that rested
in her chest
it was here
her mind took over
and told her
she was enough
she was always
enough

Black Sheep

It was quiet here
and at times I thought
I had to take control
and do everything myself
but I realized
it was safe to ask for help
it was safe
to tell my story
the way I truly lived it

Wattney Lander

" I didn't want to call you
while I was drowning
I didn't want to pull you down with me"

I said

"I'll hold your hand
no matter the depth"

- best friends

Black Sheep

Sometimes
you have to walk back
to the house you grew up in
to show yourself
it's not your home
anymore

Wattney Lander

Go baby girl
find the light
you're meant to hold
find the darkness
you're meant to go through
and find yourself
waiting for you

Black Sheep

When you go searching for the truth
sometimes you find things
you weren't looking for
sometimes
you find you

Wattney Lander

I just want you to know
you don't have to hold the hands
of your past ghosts
you're free to expand
the way you wish

Black Sheep

If they're constantly
pointing fingers at others
it just means
they're too afraid
to face themselves

Today
I have chosen
to stop holding the hands
of those who refuse
to walk forward with me
their emotions
aren't mine to carry
their paths
aren't mine to take
I am choosing
to transform and shift
the way my energy desires
regardless of those
who tell me
I am wrong
or what is right

Black Sheep

Maybe they didn't show up
but you did
and sometimes
that's all
that matters

Wattney Lander

I welcomed death
when I witnessed
my mind and body
crumble away
all the lies

- evolving

Black Sheep

Look how far you've come
how much you've fallen
how much you've risen

look how long you've lived
how much you've seen
how much you've learned

look how deep you've loved
how much you've felt
how much you've received

- it's not over yet

Wattney Lander

I felt as if
I was guided here
to be in this moment
with mother nature
to show me
that all things we hold on to
out of fear
are okay to let go of
and how beautiful
and necessary it is
for life to grow
and prosper

Black Sheep

Escaping a truth
that you once belonged to
not only takes great courage
but a great amount of love
for yourself
because it's not easy
leaving behind
a place where you thought
you received your love the most
and walking into a future
of plenty of unknowns

Wattney Lander

Sometimes
we look to others
for answers
when most of the time
those answers we seek
and need
can be found within ourselves
and they've been there
all along
you just have to dig
dig deep

Black Sheep

Give yourself
the space to explore
and be curious

stay close and connected
when tears start to fall

and allow yourself
to find you
the way you want
and need to

Wattney Lander

Don't rush your time being lost
find that ocean and really feel it
take you back and forth
accept it's challenges and surrender
to it's madness
it will push you
to where you're meant to be
and slowly
you'll start finding
what you need
to bring you back
to shore

Black Sheep

Open your hands
the world you want
is right before you
let it come in
let yourself go

Wattney Lander

Crumble your walls
release the unwanted parts
you've been holding of yourself
understand that this type of death
should happen
in order to see
there is truly no death
after all

Black Sheep

Your soul is emerging
and with time
this is how
you'll put yourself
back together

Wattney Lander

She danced
in the fields
filled with fog
for she knew
embracing her clouds
was the first step
to feeling home

Black Sheep

The only time
I ever looked back
was when I was ready
to forgive myself
for casting my past
in a negative light
instead of thanking it
for my future steps

Wattney Lander

It's within the silence
we learn
the most
about each other

Black Sheep

An amazing thing
about children
is as they grow
they ask their parents
to do the same
but only some
choose to do the work
while others refuse it

"Mommy, why do leaves fall?"

"To start again, my love"

- morning walks

Black Sheep

She was brave
and just like the sun
she kept rising
even on the days
the clouds covered
her light

Wattney Lander

They're proud of you
it's just their ego
is in the way

Black Sheep

Surrendering
doesn't mean you're weak
surrendering means
you're wise for accepting
what is
and strong enough to trust
what will be

Wattney Lander

Walk next to those
who push you forward
instead of the ones
who enjoy
pulling you back

Black Sheep

I sit in peace
knowing that what happened
only surfaced because of your rotten roots
it wasn't your fault
you were never made to feel
seen, heard or loved
you were acting out
what you were taught
and were told
"that's how we love someone"

and now
I am here to teach you

THIS is how we love
THIS is how we give
THIS is how we're made
to feel safe

- generations

Wattney Lander

You have woken up
and if no one has told you already
I am proud of you

Continue to stand as you are
bruised, bent or scarred
wilted, stuck or bloomed
and know that there are others out there
just like you

We are never alone
we're all connected
whether it be in this lifetime
or many others before this one

I see you're strong, courageous and brave
for deciding to go on this journey of self-healing
and I send you a warm hug of love and success

- I hear you. I see you. I commend you.

I am with you

ABOUT THE AUTHOR

Wattney Lander was born and raised in Ontario, Canada, where she lives with her husband and their three children. She has written poetry for over ten years, with *'**Black Sheep**"* being her first published book.

When she isn't writing, she is exploring forest trails, sitting with her kids in a botanical garden or having an in-depth conversation about the spirit world.

Follow her on Instagram or TikTok @wattneypoetry

Check out more books written by Wattney
over at **www.wattneypoetry.com**